WHERE THE DANK MEMES ARE

By Ellie Gaunt

NOT FOR CHILDREN'S BOOKS

Where The Dank Memes Are

First published by Hungry Wolf Press 2024
www.hungrywolf.net

A catalogue record of this book is available from the British Library
Library of Congress Cataloging-in-Publication Data Available
ISBN-13: 978-1-917595-12-4 | Paperback

Max sat on his mossy throne, wearing his crown sideways like a boss, scrolling through his WildPad™. Around him, the Wild Things danced, roared, and reposte Max, the Boy King of Dank Memes, sat on his mossy gaming throne, bored out of his skull. His throne was rotten. He'd carved it himself from jungle wood, and now it stank of mildew and something sharp, something sour, like it was sweating in the heat. The headset-crown on his head was heavier each day, pressing like guilt. Around him, the Wild Things danced their rumpus, replaying the same tired memes: a cat dancing, a baby laughing, a decades-old keyboard smash. It all felt stale, empty, dead.

"This is all the same!" Max growled, flinging his tablet into the mud. "Rage comics? Dancing babies? Lame!"

The Wild Things wailed and roared and gnashed their teeth. Days turned to weeks. That's when the whispers began.

"Kurt's gone," said a horned one, trembling.

"He said we weren't wild enough," growled another, its yellow eyes glassy and reddening from sleep deprivation. "He wanted to find the dark things. He wanted to be free."

Max froze. "Gone? Gone where?"

"To the Far Web," said a creature with a too-wide smile. "He said he was looking for something danker."

"The Far Web?" Max barked. "No one goes there." Max laughed, sharp and loud, the way you laugh when you're scared.

"He wanted something darker," another creature murmured, its fur patchy. "Something...dank. Something real."

Max slammed his sceptrepad against the ground, the metallic echo ringing like an error message. "I'm the king of memes!" he roared. "If Kurt thinks he can out-dank me, I'll show him who's king of lulz!"

The Wild Things roared in approval, but their voices sounded thin. Some of them were already shuffling back to their devices.

So Max grabbed his crooked crown, stepped into his incognito browserboat, typed in the forbidden URL, and began his descent into the Far Web. As he set off, leaving the hollow cheers of Wild Things behind, he thought he heard something else beneath their cheers. A faint, low growl from the jungle itself.

The river glitched and shimmered with shifting pixels, its surface alive with static and rainbow fractals. The air buzzed with corrupted audio: faint voices whispering, faint screams cut short. Pop-up ads flickered in and out like predatory fireflies: "Hot singles in your area!" "Earn $10,000 working from home!" "Click here and never log off!"

Max could hear the river moving, slurping against the muddy banks, gurgling like a throat swallowing something whole.

The trees leaned over the water, their branches clawing at each other in slow, deliberate jerks, as if they were alive but pretending not to be. From somewhere deep in the jungle came a sound: a wet crunch, followed by a scream that started loud and shrill but broke off too fast, leaving only silence.

Max paddled deeper, his oars splashing through waves that rippled like liquid code. The jungle closed in around him, its trees gnarled and twisting, their leaves glowing faintly like loading screens.

Max shuddered, gripping his sceptrepad tighter. A low chuckle echoed from the trees, a sound like corrupted audio, stuttering and broken. "Kurt's just playing," Max whispered, though his voice faltered. "I'm the king," he whispered to himself. "I'm the dankest of all.

The river hissed back at him, glitching softly in the dark. A thick mist rolled off the water, curling into the boat like a living thing. It stank—hot and sour, like rotting meat left in the sun. Max coughed, then stopped when he thought he heard laughter, high and breathy, coming from nowhere and everywhere at once.

On the second day, Max found the first signs of Kurt's handiwork. Wild Things chained to trees, their claws filed down to bloody nubs. They whispered prayer-like slogans in a language Max didn't understand.

He drifted past a flickering banner that hovered above the river like a spectral ad:

"Welcome to Kurt's Kingdom: Where the Dank Things Are!"

Below it lay a heap of corrupted gifs. A once-laughing baby now twitched, its loop frozen in a grimace. A pixelated frog stared blankly at the sky, its face warped beyond recognition. The smell hit Max like a slap—hot plastic, burnt circuits, and something rancid beneath it, like wet fur left to decompose.

Wild Things crouched, tied to rotting posts with vines of sparking wires. Their fur was matted with mud, their eyes dull and lifeless. Some whimpered, their mouths looping the same words over and over: "Kurt is everything. Kurt is hunger. Kurt is content. Kurt is dank."

Max stepped ashore, his boots sinking into the glitched mud. He found a crude totem made of keyboards and shattered screens, wrapped in thorny wires. A crown of jagged pixels sat atop it, glowing faintly with green static.

"Kurt," Max called, his voice shaking.

A guttural voice rasped back: "Kurt is everything. Kurt is... content."

Max recoiled, the smell of rot thick in his nose. He stumbled back into the boat and pushed off, his breath coming in gasps.

"Just a game," he muttered, though his voice shook. "Kurt's just... playing a game."

The jungle seemed to laugh at him. A deep, rumbling chuckle that made the air vibrate.

Behind him, the river whispered again, louder this time: a distorted gurgling laugh, looping endlessly.

The deeper Max rowed, the more the jungle changed. The trees grew closer together, their roots writhing like snakes amongst incompatible cables in the muck. Trees with glowing, pixelated bark loomed overhead, their branches clutching the sky like frozen loading wheels. The ground pulsed with faint static, vines of tangled code sparking and twitching as they crawled over rocks and roots.

The air was thick, heavy with the stench of overheated servers and scorched plastic. Somewhere above, something screeched, a sound too high, too sharp, that felt like it was slicing into Max's skull.

And the voices. Always the voices. Faint and whispering, rising and falling like waves of corrupted audio: "Like... Share... Subscribe..."

Max gritted his teeth and pushed on. "Kurt's just playing a game," he muttered, but the jungle wasn't playing.

And then came the whispers. A new type of content.

At first, Max thought it was the wind, but the voices grew louder, closer, rasping like claws on stone. They didn't speak words. Just sounds, low and guttural, dripping with meaning Max didn't want to understand. He decided to take a break, he'd been holding the sceptrepad for hours and it was beginning to singe his skin.

Then, all at once, the jungle came alive. The Wild Rumpus.

A single, sharp glitch echoed through the jungle like a shattering file, and the Wild Things burst forth. They emerged from the shadows and from screens embedded in the bark of trees, their fur rippling with static, their faces twisted into warped, too-human smiles. They howled in jagged audio bursts—discordant, looping noises that twisted Max's stomach. Their movements lagged and then snapped into place, their claws slashing at the air with unnatural precision.

They didn't just dance, they tore. Trees groaned as they splintered to the ground, their glowing leaves scattering like dying pixels. The ground cracked open, spewing waves of tangled code that wrapped around the Wild Things like ribbons, only to be shredded in their frenzy.

Max found himself caught in the chaos, swept into the Rumpus as the Wild Things grabbed at him with claws of raw data and hands made of corrupted files. He stumbled and laughed and screamed, his crown knocked sideways as he tried to roar above the noise.

The jungle shrieked in protest as it flattened under their frenzy. Trees fell like dominoes. The river spilled over its banks, static pouring onto the ground in shimmering floods. The sky itself flickered, the bruised purples and golds collapsing into empty black, as if the whole world was buffering.

"Enough!" Max roared, planting his sceptrepad into the ground. The sound of his voice echoed, breaking through the noise like a final, piercing error alert. The Wild Things froze, their heads jerking toward him in unnatural, glitchy snaps.

For a moment, silence fell, thick and heavy. Max adjusted his crown and whispered under his breath: "Kurt's just playing a game."

But in the static-filled void, the jungle growled back, its voice low and seething: The game is playing you.

Max's boat finally scraped to a halt on the shore of Kurt's fortress—a massive, twitching structure of neon screens and broken monitors. It writhed with movement, Wild Things crawling up and down like ants, their eyes hollow, their fur falling out in patches. They carried stones, broken monitors and ex-crypto mining GPUs to the base, piling them higher and higher, as if trying to reach the moon. Within the debris, bones, skulls, and bits of fur. The air hung with the stink of stale testosterone. Glowing pop-ups flickered across its walls: "All Content, All the Time." Above the gate, another banner:

"Enter if you Dare, Stay if You Don't."

Inside, Wild Things shuffled aimlessly, their faces replaced with warped, hollowed-out screens. Some stared at looping memes on giant monitors, their bodies slumped as if drained. Others wandered, their clawed hands dragging across the ground, mumbling, "Kurt... Kurt..."

And there, on a throne made of tangled wires and shattered glass, sat Kurt.

Kurt was enormous now, his fur matted with blood and sap and streaked with corrupted files. His claws longer than Max's sceptrepad. Atop his head sat a glittering crown, a jagged halo of sparking code, composed of rare NFTs and one-time-only Twitch drops. His eyes glowed an unnatural green in the darkness, flickering with static.

"Max," Kurt said, his voice Auto-Tuned and hollow. "You came."

Max stepped forward, his knees shaking. "Kurt," he said, his voice cracking. "I'm here to bring you back."

"Back?" Kurt laughed—a sound like trees snapping in a storm. "There's nothing to go back to. This is where I belong. This is where we belong. You can get anything you want here in the Far Web. Anything."

Max pointed his sceptrepad at Kurt. "You're not a king. You're not that dank. You're just playing, pretending!"

He climbed the tower, slipping on broken meme templates and discarded hashtags. His heart pounding like a jungle drum machine. When he reached the top, Kurt leaned forward, his green, flickering eyes boring into Max. "Oh, Max," he said softly. "You still don't get it, do you? You didn't come here to out-dank me. You came here because you're afraid."

"I'm not afraid!" Max shouted, but his voice trembled.

"You're afraid of what you are," Kurt growled. "You called yourself king of the memes. You made them bow. You made them roar for you, share you over and over. And now you're running from it."

Kurt grabbed Max's headset-crown and held it high. "This? This is yours, isn't it? This stupid little headset. You told them to love you. To fear you. You turned them into... griefers and trolls."

Kurt returned the crown to Max and gave his nose a "boop."

"No!" Max screamed. "That's not true!"

But it was. He saw it now—saw himself stomping and roaring, pointing his sceptrepad, giving orders. He'd called it a game, but it wasn't. It had never been a game.

"I came to bring you back!" Max snapped, though his voice cracked. "This isn't real. None of this is real!"

Kurt laughed, a deep, stuttering sound that made the air vibrate. "Oh, it's real, Max. Realer than anything you've ever seen. I've found the true nature of memes. They don't make you laugh. They take you. They eat you."

"You're lying!" Max shouted.

"Images, millions of images, that's what I eat."

Kurt stood, towering over Max, his grin widened, his teeth sharp as shattered pixels. "The glitch jungle doesn't lie, Max. It shows you what you are." Kurt laughed, deep and terrible. "You didn't come here to save me, Max. You came here because you are me."

Max froze. For a moment, he saw himself reflected in Kurt's glowing eyes. His crown, his sceptrepad, his snarling face—they weren't Kurt's. They were his.

Max turned and ran, his boots slipping on shards of glass and bones and gaming merch. He tumbled down the tower, the Wild Things below reaching for him with bony claws. Behind him, Kurt's laughter echoed through the jungle, shaking the trees, stuttering and looping like a corrupted file.

"You can't escape, Max!" Kurt roared. "The memes are in you. They've always been in you!"

Max dove into his boat, shoving it off into the river of static. Behind him, the fortress began to collapse, its walls flickering and crumbling into glowing fragments.

The river carried him away, faster and faster, as Kurt's laughter faded into the endless hum of servers, a background noise that never goes away.

Max's boat drifted back to the shore of his old kingdom, where the Wild Things were waiting, hopeful and desperate for new memes, new content. Their devices clutched in their claws, their eyes wide and hungry.

"Did you find Kurt?" they asked.

Max dropped his headset-crown into the mud. "I found him," he said quietly. "And he's staying there."

The Wild Things howled, but Max didn't join them. He turned and walked away, leaving the devices and the kingdom behind. He walked into the forest, the jungle's whispers still echoing in his mind.

But in his pocket, his device buzzed with a new notification.

And somewhere, in the depths of the digital jungle, Kurt's laughter glitched on.

Maurice Sendak once said he felt all his other books lived in the shadow of Where the Wild Things Are. In Tell Them Anything You Want (Spike Jonze and Lance Bangs, 2009), a documentary released shortly before his death, Sendak reflected on his life with a mix of wit and grumpiness, admitting that while Wild Things made him famous, he had a soft spot for the books no one remembered—In the Night Kitchen, Outside Over There. The ones that didn't make T-shirts or lunchboxes.

And that's the cruel truth about creativity today: it's all shadows and chasing. Except now, instead of chasing meaning, we're chasing metrics. Virality. The sweet, addictive high of relevance. But memes don't last. They're chewed up and spat out by the machine, faster than a Wild Rumpus could flatten a forest.

Where the Dank Memes Are is our twisted tribute to both Sendak's wildness and the modern artist's endless, grotesque consumption of likes, trends, and meaningless engagement. To achive this, we combined it with Joseph Conrad's Heart of Darkness. It's what happens when you feed the algorithm so much you become part of it. A cautionary tale for anyone who's ever felt the dark pull of the next post, the next hit, the next meme.

What did I just read?

You have just read a reimagined children's book from Hungry Wolf Press' "Not For Children's" series. As it says on the tin, these stories are NOT for children. In fact they are barely fit for human consumption. They are written by a fictious person called Ellie Gaunt. Ellie is a pen name, they are part of the Hungry Wolf Pack, a collective of weird and wonderfully wacky writers who aim to create stories that make you want to Howl at the moon. We all wear the Three Wolf Moon T-shirt as our uniform, so we are utterly brilliant and ace at everything. But we also use lots of computers and this book was written in collaboration with Kerouac, our resident AI*. Kerouac is trained on open-source materials and a large corpus of our own published and unpublish(able) writing. We believe it is Fair Trained, but it is also trained on the tears of small children, the laughter of bullies in the night, the sound of vomit hitting the tiles at 3am, and some other spinny stuff. So we apologise that what you read can hardly qualify as human writing, but we hope you enjoyed it nonetheless.

*We use multiple custom Large Language Models to produce the writing in these works. One is ChatGPT-4o, featuring a custom GPT trained on a corpus of Hungry Wolf Writers. We also use an offline model running Stability AI's open-source models and Ollama, again trained on the Howls of the Wolf Pack. Most stories are fleshed out from prompts and then put through several LLMs to generate the text, then they are edited by human minds which are just as warped as the machines. For some books we use DALL-E but most are done with Midjourney. Prompts are taken through several draft versions and edits before being sent to our art dept. who tweak out the most obvious AI fails by hand. However, our art team, like all our writers, don't actually exist so not everything we print is perfect, but we try to make products at the quality-level they deserve (meme aesthetic, yeah?). And that's about it. If you read all this and are just fascinated to know more and more and more, then follow the tracks to hungrywolf.net and sign up to get precious intel whenever we hatch another scheme.

About Where The Dank Memes Are
This work is a parody inspired by themes from classic children's literature but aimed squarely at adult audiences. Where the Dank Memes Are takes its initial cue from Maurice Sendak's Where the Wild Things Are, a story that became a cultural juggernaut, casting a long shadow over Sendak's career. While Wild Things celebrated the untamed wilderness of childhood imagination, our version dives headfirst into the glitchy, neon jungle of meme culture, where chaos reigns, and creativity is swallowed by algorithms.

This parody is entirely distinct from the original. Its text, structure, and illustrations have been reinterpreted and transformed into a surreal critique of the digital age. Through humor, absurdity, and existential dread, it examines the relentless pursuit of relevance and the modern artist's endless quest for the next viral moment.

Where the Dank Memes Are doesn't reproduce Sendak's text or illustrations but instead serves as a satirical homage, twisting its themes into a reflection of today's content-driven madness. It's not a replacement for Where the Wild Things Are—how could it be?—but a warped funhouse mirror that asks: what happens when our inner wildness meets the digital void?

www.ingramcontent.com/pod-product-compliance
Lightning Source LLC
LaVergne TN
LVHW071133160826
845679LV00005B/1264
9781917595124